DEVOTIONS FOR CAREGIVERS

A Month's Supply of Prayer

Marilyn Driscoll

Paulist Press
New York/Mahwah, N.J.

Cover design by Cynthia Dunne

Library of Congress Cataloging-in-Publication Data

Driscoll, Marilyn.
    Devotions for caregivers : a month's supply of prayer / Marilyn Driscoll.
        p. cm.—(IlluminationBook)
    ISBN 0-8091-4394-1 (alk. paper)
    1. Caregivers—Prayer-books and devotions—English. I. Title. II. Illumination-Books.
    BV4910.9.D75 2006
    242'.68—dc22

                                                                        2006002749

Published by Paulist Press
997 Macarthur Boulevard
Mahwah, New Jersey 07430

www.paulistpress.com

Printed and bound in the
United States of America

Contents

A Note of Introduction

Whether you are the caregiver because you are a family member or friend, or whether caregiving is your profession–in hospital, nursing home, or private home–there are days when a short break to think and pray can be "just what the doctor ordered"–for you. This little book may help!

DAY 1
Interrupted Rest

*I*n Mark 6, verse 31, Jesus invited his disciples to "...come with me by yourselves to a quiet place and get some rest."

READ MARK 6:30–44.

Jesus recognized the need his followers were feeling for some rest. Yet even this time of rest was interrupted by the greater needs of the crowd of people. And because Jesus was compassionate, he ministered to their needs before his own.

If you are a caregiver, you know how much you need a time of rest, of refreshment. You long for a quiet place where at least for a while no one will be making demands on you. How difficult it is sometimes even to have a normal night's sleep.

1

When God took on human flesh and lived among us as Jesus, God with us, he shared in these human needs. There are two places in Scripture where we are told, "Jesus sighed" (Mark 7:34 and 8:12). What an interesting detail to be included in the Bible! God must have known there would be a time it would help us to know that Jesus sighed. God makes no mistakes about the details he includes in his Word!

Oh Lord, thank you for becoming one of us. Thank you for sharing some of the same human feelings that I experience. Help me, Lord, to draw the strength I need today from your Holy Spirit, who lives in me.

Stop for a minute. Sigh. Tell the Lord why you are sighing, if you know why you are sighing! Perhaps in the sigh you can exhale some of the heaviness you have been holding within you. Make room for the Holy Spirit to occupy that space, to fill you with God's love and compassion.

A Sigh

Lord Jesus, You sighed!
Were You, like I, tired?
What a fact to record
Of our Savior and Lord,
To remember that sound
And write such a thing down.
I read it today
On my own troubled way
And it gives me new hope
As I wearily cope.
With God's Spirit within
A sigh is not sin.

DAY 2
Clothed in Compassion

*P*aul advised the Christians at Colossae to "clothe yourselves with compassion, kindness, humility, gentleness and patience" (Col 3:12).

READ COLOSSIANS 3:12–17.

If you are a caregiver, you know how important compassion and kindness are to those who look to you for the care and services they need.

The vulnerability of someone who is sick or disabled, frail, very old, or very young is evident. This kind of vulnerability highlights the importance of a gentle physical touch, a hand to hold when one is afraid, a hug after a dangerous situation. The vulnerability of need seeks a smile, a kind word, sometimes some humor.

If you are a caregiver because a family member needs care, sometimes it is necessary to reclothe yourself with the kindness and compassion mentioned in this verse of Scripture. Caregivers get tired and worn, and a look into a mirror can be a reminder that the garments of gentleness or patience have worn thin. God provides new garments to his people. Discard the worn garment of impatience, or the garment of harsh thoughts, or the garment of pride. God provides new, clean garments. Take a minute to discard the old and put on the new.

If you are a caregiver not because your own family member or friend needs you, but because this is your profession, your calling, your job, God also gives you the garment of compassion—perhaps in extra measure because you need it as you minister to people you do not know. The "kindness of strangers" is often commented on after a time of difficulty, danger, illness, or emergency. God provides the ability to be kind and compassionate in the work we do.

Father, thank you that you allow us to call you "Our Father." We thank you for this family relationship. Help me, Lord, to live and act as part of a loving family, offering compassion and kindness and patience to others in your name.

Stop for a minute. Think about God's love for you. Think about God's love for the person for whom you provide care. Thank God that you are there to represent God's love to that person—that you can be the gentle touch of Jesus to someone.

present temporary world into a place and condition so much better that it is not worth trying to make a comparison. Please continue to encourage me from your word.

Stop for a minute. Think of your own hurts and struggles. Think of the hurts and struggles of the person you take care of. Think of some of the ways God has provided help and encouragement in an unexpected way. Another person may be the answer to your present need. And you may be the answer to another's need. Even in this way, God makes things work together for good.

DAY 4
Cushioned Care

*E*bed-Melech the Cushite said to Jeremiah, "Put these rags and worn-out clothes under your arms to pad the ropes" *(Jer 38:12).*

READ JEREMIAH 38:6–13 AND 39:15–18.

A foreigner who worked for King Zedekiah was instrumental in rescuing the prophet Jeremiah from the deep pit in which he had been imprisoned. It would have been heroic enough for Ebed-Melech to successfully rescue Jeremiah. How praiseworthy that this man, a foreigner, perhaps a slave, was concerned about God's prophet.

But Ebed-Melech went a step further. He figured out a way to help Jeremiah with an added comfort, a kindness that took a little more thought and planning and effort. To cushion the prophet's armpits when lifting him out of the pit with ropes, he had someone find and bring some old rags. What a surprising detail to be included in this biblical narrative. Isn't God's Word wonderful! How wise of God to tell us about this detail.

If you are a caregiver and responsible for the basic needs of someone who cannot help himself or herself, you may have opportunities to provide a little extra comfort above and beyond the basic need. A little extra thought and planning can mean a lot to someone else—as it did to Jeremiah.

It is also interesting to note in Jeremiah 39 that Ebed-Melech was rewarded. He was allowed to escape the fate of the rest of the city. But it doesn't say he was rewarded because he rescued Jeremiah or because he thoughtfully provided the cushion under the ropes. It says he was rewarded because his heart was right toward God.

Lord, I ask you to direct me in what I do, in the way I do it, and in the motives of my heart. Make my heart right with you.

Stop for a minute. Think about this obscure biblical character. Perhaps, like him, you are a stranger in the country where you are working. Perhaps you feel obscure and unnoticed. Are there ways in which an extra act of kindness would make a big difference to someone's comfort and well-being?

DAY 5
Examples to Imitate

We know from the Bible that God gives Christians the power of his Holy Spirit within them to enable them to live a Christian life. We do not live "Christianly" by our own power or effort. This could lead one to think that observing another Christian's example or imitating what we see another person doing does not fit into God's method for our Christian growth and sanctification. But the Bible says otherwise.

READ 1 CORINTHIANS 4:16; 1 THESSALONIANS 1:6 AND 2:14; AND HEBREWS 6:12 AND 13:7.

Do you notice in these verses phrases such as "imitate me" and "imitators of us and of the Lord"? In Hebrews the emphasis is on imitating those who were good examples of faith. There's another verse (Ephesians 5:1) that tells us to be "imitators of God."

These verses lead me to believe that as we live the Christian life (not possible without the power of God's Holy Spirit), we still need the supporting examples of other Christians. And, sobering thought, we *are* those "other Christians" to someone looking at us as an example. Our teaching and learning by example are part of the Holy Spirit's plan and method; they are not in opposition to it.

I may protest that I am "just doing my job as a caregiver," that I never asked to be an example to anyone else. Nevertheless this is one of the ways God uses to teach his people how to live out their lives of faith, love, patience, and wisdom in this difficult world. Not only are nonbelievers watching us to say "Aha!" when we slip and fall, but believers are watching us to be encouraged in their walk.

Lord, these thoughts give me even more reason to depend on you for your power within me. Thank you that you do not leave us alone in the world, wondering what to do and how to do it. Thank you for your ample guidance and wisdom. Open my eyes to see and learn.

Stop for a minute. Think again about those verses in Matthew 11, "Come unto me all ye that labor and are heavy laden, and I will give you rest. Take my yoke upon you, and learn of me; for I am meek and lowly in heart: and ye shall find rest unto your souls. For my yoke is easy and my burden is light" (Matt 11:28-30 KJV). Of the many things we are to learn about Jesus, here we are directed to concentrate on his "meek and lowly of heart" characteristics—apparently an essential attitude for us if we are to be lightened and find rest for our own souls.

DAY 6
What Are Friends For?

*J*esus was speaking to a crowd in a friend's house. Suddenly there was noise and falling dirt and then light streaming from the ceiling. Someone was removing the tiles from the roof, and next a man on a stretcher was being lowered from the roof into the room where Jesus was speaking. Jesus' reputation had been spreading—this man from God had the ability to heal people! The paralytic's friends did not want to miss the opportunity to bring their disabled friend to Jesus to ask for his healing touch.

READ LUKE 5:17–26.

If you are a caregiver, you have probably wished for a miracle. You may have brought the needs of your patient to God in prayer, asking him to heal if it is his will, or to lessen pain, or to change a harmful attitude.

If you are a caregiver because it is your relative or friend who needs you, your prayers may have been coming up to God on many occasions over a long period of time.

If you are a caregiver because this is your calling and profession, your knowledge of this patient's needs may be new and your prayers to date infrequent.

Prayer is always proper. Jesus touched people and they were healed. Sometimes even today God will break into what seems like a hopeless situation and will bring about a healing that can only be considered miraculous. Usually the many means of medicine, doctors, surgery, recovery time, exercise, and patience are the ways by which God touches the ill and infirm today. But it is always proper to pray, to ask God for his touch in whatever way and at whatever time he chooses. Sometimes God's touch is his way of saying "Come home now." Death becomes life eternal because it is God's ultimate healing.

Lord, please give me the kind of faith the friends of the paralytic evidenced when they brought their friend to Jesus. Help me to believe that you can do anything and that you will do what is right in each circumstance. I thank you that you are such a powerful God that you forgive sins today, even as you did long ago.

Stop for a minute. Consider what a marvelous gift our faith is. Think of the words, "...by grace are [you] saved through faith; and that not of yourselves: it is the gift of God" (Eph 2:8 KJV). Use your faith to bring the weak and needy into Jesus' presence.

DAY 7
Wisdom from God

*S*ometimes we have to make a lot of decisions, some of them seemingly easy, others difficult. They may be about lifestyle changes, changes in location, medical choices, or financial matters. The decisions we have been accustomed to making day by day become natural and somewhat automatic, but when we run up against some new area or potentially life-changing decision, we are reminded how much we need wisdom. This is especially true when the decision we are making affects another person.

READ JAMES 1:5–8 AND 3:13–18.

The Book of James first tells us that any person has God's permission to ask him for wisdom. We have permission, and we are encouraged and urged to do so. But when we ask for wisdom we need to have a basic reliance on God so that we can recognize and accept the wisdom he gives without doubting it.

But how can we know what God's wisdom is? In the third chapter of James he tells us about characteristics of the wrong kind of wisdom (earthly or devilish) and those of the right kind of wisdom. The wisdom guiding any decision needs to be tested against the criteria listed here: pure, peace-loving, considerate, submissive, full of mercy and good fruit, impartial, and sincere (James 3:17).

If you are a caregiver, you know you are sometimes called upon to make decisions in unfamiliar areas. Isn't it reassuring that you can ask God for wisdom and he will answer that prayer? Stay tuned in to God's Word, the Bible, in order to recognize what his wisdom looks like.

Oh Lord, thank you for promising to give us the wisdom we need to do the work you have called us to do. Thank you for reminding me that I am to ask for that wisdom, and thank you that difficult decisions can cause me to turn to you for help.

Stop for a minute. Can you remember the last time you delayed a decision in order to consult with God about something you were about to do? God knows that we are frail and forgetful, and he is gracious to remind us that he is alongside us and able to help us.

DAY 8
Odd Advice

When I was taking care of my aging parents their pastor once said to me, "Remember, no matter how much you do, you'll still feel guilty." What kind of pastoral advice was this? Although I wondered about this when I first heard his words, over time these words from a seasoned and experienced pastor proved to be words of wisdom.

READ ROMANS 5:5 AND 13:8.

When the Holy Spirit convicts of sin, righteousness, and judgment (John 16:8), that conviction produces guilt, which, in a way, is God's gracious way of showing us our need of him and his forgiveness. This is true guilt, and we would not wish it away until it has done its work in bringing us to the one who saves from sin. But there is also a false guilt that dogs our steps even after we have confessed our sins to the Lord and accepted his grace and forgiveness.

If you are a caregiver for parents or grandparents or other elderly seniors in your family, or for others whose lives have impacted you through the years, feelings that much resemble feelings of guilt may hover over you only because the "debt of love" can never be repaid. Just as we cannot pay our "debt" to God for his free gift, we also cannot pay the "debt of love" to those who loved us.

If you are a professional caregiver, sometimes the loving care you offer to your patient will remind you of the love you shared with members of your own family. God is gracious in allowing love to spill over into other relationships.

Lord, I thank you for the love you spread abroad in our hearts. It is more than comes naturally to us, though that kind of love is also important. You are gracious and generous with your people, and you always know what we need. Thank you.

Stop for a minute. Remember some of the people who loved you but who are no longer living. Perhaps you remember their faults and shortcomings, which were present along with their love. God can give you the ability to forgive them, even now.

Give Me a Break

*M*artha *and Mary are famous sisters. Even people who don't read the Bible are probably familiar with these two women: Martha, who was busy with housework and cooking, and Mary, who preferred to sit and listen to the guest of honor, Jesus.*

R EAD L UKE 10:38–42.

Are you a Martha or a Mary?

There is surely a need for both Marthas and Marys in the world. Jesus said that listening to him was a better choice. The role of housework and cleanup and cooking looks like harder work than sitting next to Jesus and listening to his teaching. This is true, but only sometimes. There are other times when we know we need to sit next to Jesus and listen to him, but we are afraid of what he might tell us, what he might ask us or ask us to do. Those times it's easier to stick to the housework and let someone else talk to Jesus.

If you are a caregiver, you know how involved you can be in the daily chores of your job, taking care of the personal needs of your patient as well as cleaning, cooking, and straightening up. Remember, when there's an opportunity to spend even a few minutes talking to Jesus or listening to Jesus, try to take full advantage of that opportunity.

Lord, I thank you for all the abilities that you have given me. Thank you for hands that can serve you. Thank you for a mind that can remember and think and reason. Thank you for feet and legs strong enough to get me where I need to go, for eyes that see and ears that hear. Especially, I thank you that you have given me your Holy Spirit so that I can comprehend the spiritual truths you want to teach me.

Stop for a minute. Sit down. Close your eyes. Imagine you are in the same room with Jesus. He is saying these words to you, "Come to me all you who labor and are heavy laden and I will give you rest. Take my yoke upon you and learn of me for I am meek and lowly of heart and you will find rest for your souls. For my yoke is easy and my burden is light" (Matt 11:28–30 KJV). Answer him. "Here I am. I come. I am glad to be connected to you. I am willing to learn from you what it means to have a lowly heart."

DAY 10
A Get-Well Card

*S*trengthen you with power...in your inner being....[P]ower...to grasp how wide and long and high and deep is the love of Christ...(who is able to do immeasurably more than all we ask or imagine).

God's power can be at work in people!

READ EPHESIANS 3:14–21.

Sometimes instead of sending a "store-bought" get-well card, I use some blank notepaper and write out the verses that the words above come from, the third chapter of Ephesians (verses 16 and 18). Especially when the person (whose body is failing) is someone who has, for a long time, walked closely with God, these words encourage me as the sender of the card. Of course I hope they also encourage the person to whom I am sending the card. Following St. Paul's example, we can pray for that person's inner spiritual strength and power.

If you are a caregiver, you may have spent time taking care of a person whose inner spiritual strength and power seemed to be much greater than his or her physical condition warranted. Take joy in the immeasurable power and love of God. The unexpected spiritual strength you witnessed may have been a result of someone's prayers for that person.

Lord, I pray that you will, even now, reveal your wider, longer, higher, deeper love to someone who needs it most, and that you will work your strong power in the heart and mind and soul of that person.

Stop for a minute. Read again the words in Ephesians 3 and make those words of Scripture your personal prayer for a specific person whose inner being will benefit from spiritual strength and power. Let God use your prayers.

DAY 11
Behold Your Mother

*T*he words that are recorded that Jesus spoke while he hung on the cross are especially meaningful to us. Suffering human need, he cried, "I thirst." He cried out to his Father. He forgave those who tortured him. He assured a repenting thief of his eternal life. And, using the words noted above, before he said, "It is finished," Jesus commended his mother into the care of his beloved disciple, John.

READ JOHN 19:25–30. IF YOU HAVE TIME, ALSO READ MATTHEW 27:45–46; MARK 15:34; AND LUKE 23:39–46.

The verses from John's gospel (in the New International Version) read, "Near the cross of Jesus stood his mother, his mother's sister, Mary the wife of Clopas, and Mary of Magdala. When Jesus saw his mother there, and the disciple whom he loved standing nearby, he said to his mother, 'Dear woman, here is your son,' and to the disciple, 'Here is your mother.' From that time on, this disciple took her into his home."

If you are a caregiver you may be thinking already of the beloved disciple, John, in the often overlooked role of caregiver. John was not just Jesus' special friend and follower, not just author of several books in our New Testament, not just apostle and church leader, but also John the caregiver.

What might it have been like for John to have Mary, the mother of Jesus, resident in his home? Did they spend hours talking about Jesus, the object of their love and commitment? Did Mary share with John some childhood stories that others did not know about? We do not know why Jesus chose John for this role rather than other family members or some of the women mentioned in the text. But John's responsibility was John's privilege and joy.

Oh Lord, thank you for calling me into the particular job and task you now have me in. Help me to know the privilege and joy of serving you by serving those you send me to serve. Amen.

Stop for a minute. Can you think of any situations in which there was an unexpected caregiver role? Have you wondered why one family member and not another family member carried the responsibility? How can a "burden" be transformed into a "joy"?

DAY 12
A Time for Everything

*T*he Old Testament Book of Ecclesiastes contains some famous words about time and seasons. "There is a time for everything, and a season for every activity under heaven....a time to scatter stones and a time to gather them...."

READ ECCLESIASTES 3:1–15.

Once I attended a business seminar on time management—intended to inspire workers to work more efficiently and more productively. But I remember only one piece of advice, and I doubt it was what my boss had intended me to learn. It was this: It's OK to say, "I don't have to do that now."

If you are a caregiver, you probably have experienced times when you needlessly jumped up to do something immediately—when this was not needed. Sometimes, of course, one really must jump to respond to an emergency. But no one can do everything at once. And you don't need to. "To-do lists" need to be structured around priorities.

When I was caregiver to my aged parents, they expected me to write a check to pay every bill within an hour of the mail's delivery. This was their lifelong pattern, paying up front and promptly. But medical bills needed first to be processed by Medicare and then by an insurance company; I needed to convince my nervous parents that "we don't need to do that now." In fact, it is better to wait. Many times I explained, "If we still owe something, they will bill us again." Besides, my many responsibilities for their care required that I use the time available wisely and well, but not always in the ways they expected.

It was not always easy to reassure them that all that needed to be done would be done.

Lord, thank you that you move us through the seasons of life, providing what we need, one day at a time. You are in charge! Help me to slow down and depend on you. Help me to communicate a peaceful and calm manner to those who are anxious.

Stop for a minute. Think about times and seasons and the different behaviors (even in animals and plants) appropriate to each season. Make a list only of what you MUST do today. Make another list of things that can wait until another day. Make yet another list of all that you accomplished yesterday or last week.

DAY 13
Man of Sorrows

*A*man of sorrows *is the term the Old Testament prophet Isaiah used to describe Jesus, the Messiah whom Isaiah would not live to meet but who would walk this earth some seven hundred years later.*

READ ISAIAH 53:3–6—OR ALL OF ISAIAH 53 IF YOU HAVE TIME.

I remember weeping when I heard a radio newscaster talk about the Sunday school children who died in a bombing in Mississippi. It was 1963, and soon after this incident came the assassination of John F. Kennedy. The years of racist hatred continued. Then in 1968 Martin Luther King was shot, followed soon after by the shooting of Robert F. Kennedy. These were terrible and shocking events. We all shed tears. Somehow it is the memory of the bombing of the Mississippi Sunday school that continues to overwhelm my emotions. The tears are still near the surface. How could I bear such evil? How could I carry this kind of sorrow and still function? "It's too much, Lord!" I cried.

The words of Isaiah came to me, but in the form of a hymn: "Man of Sorrows! What a name—for the Son of God who came. Hallelujah, what a Savior!"

For a moment I was able in a new way to sense the magnitude of what Jesus did when he took upon himself the sins and sorrows of this world of human beings. I could not bear such a load. Nor could you. Only Jesus, God's perfect Son, can bear the sorrows of the human race. Yes. Hallelujah, what a Savior!

If you are a caregiver, there may be times when the sickness and pain and sorrow and troubles of other people almost overwhelm you. Yes, we are to "weep with them that weep" (Rom 12:15 KJV). But also we need to remember our limitations and turn to Jesus, who wants to carry our sorrows.

Lord, what a wonder that you are able to carry our sorrows and that you indeed do carry the sins and sorrows of this fallen world. Thank you for doing what I am unable to do, for doing what only you can do.

Stop for a minute. Are you carrying a load that is too heavy for you? Remember that Jesus bore the sins and sorrows of man. You cannot. He can. Can you imagine yourself releasing part of your load into the hands of Jesus?

DAY 14
A List of Soft Words

*N*ot every encounter is without stress. There are even encounters in which we find another person's reaction or attitude not just difficult, but irrational. God's Word has much to say about the words we use, both in the Old Testament Book of Proverbs and also in the New Testament, where the apostle James wrote about the power of the tongue.

READ PROVERBS 15:1–4 AND 16:20–24. IF YOU HAVE TIME, READ JAMES 3.

In the old King James Version, Proverbs 15:1 reads "A soft answer turneth away wrath; but grievous words stir up anger." Sometimes almost anything we say causes further irritation, and the best thing we can do is remain silent. At other times some response is called for, and we struggle for soft and gentle words to communicate something we hope will be calming and healing. Many languages have expressions of human courtesy and civility, combinations of words and sounds that can connote our intention to soothe and heal.

If you are a caregiver, you may experience times when the person you are caring for, or even a family member, is upset or agitated, perhaps with reason, perhaps without reason. It can help to practice using some of these words, and from time to time to add others to the list, so that soft words will be at hand when we need them. Some of these might be useful:

I don't think I agree, but there may be a better time to talk about it.
How do you feel about that? I think I understand how you feel.
I thought you might feel that way. I've wondered about that too.
Let's wait and see.
Perhaps. You may be right. Yes, I agree with you.
Right now you don't need to be upset.
Please, will you tell me your opinion? Thank you.

Our Father in Heaven, please help me to be sensitive to the rough places that need smoothing and to depend on you for the ability to smooth and soothe and heal, by my actions and by the words I use. And Lord, also please give me the wisdom to know when to be silent.

Stop for a minute. Think of other soft words or gentle words that you sometimes use that help another person to be calm and reassured. Jot them down for a time when you might need them.

DAY 15
Come unto Me

*J*esus spoke some very important and tender words to the people around him when he said in words now familiar to many of us: "Come unto me all ye who labor and are heavy laden and I will give you rest" (Matt 11:28 KJV).

READ MATTHEW 11:27–30.

These verses from a modern Bible translation (the New International Version) read as follows: "All things have been committed to me by my Father. No one knows the Son except the Father, and no one knows the Father except the Son and those to whom the Son chooses to reveal him. Come to me, all you who are weary and burdened, and I will give you rest. Take my yoke upon you and learn from me, for I am gentle and humble in heart, and you will find rest for your souls. For my yoke is easy and my burden is light."

At first in verse 27 it seems as though Jesus will withhold knowledge of God from all except "those to whom the Son chooses to reveal" something so special. But the verses that immediately follow are an open invitation. Anyone who wants to accept the invitation will be welcome. The invitation to know God is to come to his Son, Jesus. And if we are to enjoy the benefits of rest, we are to be "yoked" (or connected) to Jesus, walking with him, near him, learning from him—particularly his gentleness and humility of heart. Yes, there is a yoke. Yes, we will help to bear a burden. But compared to all the alternatives in the world around us, Jesus' yoke is easy and Jesus' burden is light.

Lord, I want to accept your invitation. I come to you now, asking you to teach me and walk with me. I have much to learn about you and from you. I invite you into my heart as my own Savior and my Lord. Please continue to reveal to me all that this means. Amen.

Stop for a minute. Perhaps you accepted Jesus' invitation to know him and love him and trust him a long time ago. Or perhaps you have only just now begun this close relationship to Jesus. Either way, there is reason to give thanks and praise to God. Surely he has provided in Jesus what we could never have provided for ourselves.

DAY 16
Pray with a Psalm

*S*ometimes when I read the Psalms I think about King David, who wrote so many of them. His life saw many hardships and seasons of danger, as well as escapes from enemies and difficulties with his own family members. True, his own actions were the cause of some of his troubles. Yet, he experienced a relationship with God that was real and important to him. Often in these times of trouble or danger we read in 1 Samuel and 2 Samuel that he cried out, "Bring me the ephod"—a ceremonial help used by the ancient Hebrews when crying out to God or when asking for God's specific direction. David's prayers were short and to the point in these times of urgent need.

But at other times in his life, his prayers were in the form of beautiful poetry that expressed his feelings. How good it is that we have these to read!

READ PSALM 5.

In Psalm 5, David says to God, "Listen to my cry for help...to you I pray. Morning by morning, O LORD, you hear my voice; morning by morning I lay my requests before you and wait in expectation." He prays about the dangers around him, and concludes his prayer with the words, "...let all who take refuge in you be glad; let them ever sing for joy....you bless the righteous; you surround them with your favor as with a shield."

David truly trusted God to take care of him. If you are a caregiver, you may feel the need to trust God, not only to take care of you, but to take care of the person you are responsible for. How difficult it can be when we feel the weight of a responsibility too heavy to comfortably carry. But God is our helper and he wants us to cry to him for help. Prayer can be with words, with cries, or with silence. God invites us to communicate with him, and his Word gives us examples of some of the ways David and other psalm writers prayed.

Our Father in Heaven, please forgive me for trying to do things on my own when it was your intention for me to ask you for your help. I ask you now, dear Jesus, to help me in this present job, this problem, this confusion, this situation. Amen.

Stop for a minute. Would it help you to make a list of some of the problems and concerns on your mind right now? Then, when you have a few extra minutes, use this list as a prayer list and take time to tell God about your concerns and to listen for his answer, for his direction. Perhaps he will use the Bible to direct your thinking.

A Miracle

*T*he Book of Acts is a history of the early church. The leaders were specific individuals who had seen Jesus, identified as apostles. (Paul was a special case because he had seen Jesus after the crucifixion, when Jesus appeared to him in a unique revelation. Paul was an apostle but had not been a disciple.)

The apostle Peter, however, was one of the disciples who had spent several years with Jesus, traveling with him throughout Israel, hearing his teachings, observing his actions, learning from Jesus how to pray. Peter was a man whose faith grew and who was empowered by the Holy Spirit to fill a leading role in the days of the early church. The apostles were empowered by the Holy Spirit in a special way as they performed their roles as witnesses of Jesus' life and resurrection and as proclaimers of the good news of salvation. They were the announcers of this news before it was recorded and communicated to become the holy Bible we now have.

READ ACTS 9:36–43.

The incident recorded in Acts 9 was special even in this miraculous time of early church history. In this chapter, Peter did not merely pray for Tabitha to be healed. She had already died, and Peter prayed that God would bring her back to life. And God did! It was so special an event, so unusual, so miraculous, that it is recorded in this ninth chapter of Acts. Tabitha (or Dorcas, her other name) was someone who was well known for her good works, for sewing clothing and giving it away to the needy. Other Christians had died, some of them apostles, with no miraculous intervention like this. But it pleased God to bring this one Christian woman back to her life of service and kindness in the early church. Miracles are God's business. We have no right to expect them. They are his special acts done at his pleasure in his time.

Lord, we do not ask for special miracles. We ask only for your presence in our lives now, in our immediate situations. Yet we know you are the same God who encouraged the earliest Christians and amazed their enemies with your acts, and we praise and thank you for who you are. Encourage me now in your own way.

Stop for a minute. Do you think there are ways in which God intervenes today in our lives and problems? In what ways are these interventions "miracles"? In what ways has God encouraged you?

DAY 18
A List of Fruit

*T*he Bible contains a number of useful lists, summaries of qualities or characteristics that are guidelines for Christians on how to live. One such list is the "fruit of the spirit" that Paul summarized for the Christian church in Galatia to review.

READ GALATIANS 5, ESPECIALLY VERSES 16–23.

Earlier in Galatians 5 a list of the "works of the flesh" (KJV) is detailed, mentioning such things as adultery, fornication, idolatry, witchcraft, hatred, violence, strife, and heresies. About these conditions and modes of behavior Paul says, "those who live like this will not inherit the kingdom of God" (Gal 5:21 NIV). In sharp contrast to this unpleasant list is the list of the fruit of the Spirit. In the King James translation these are "…love, joy, peace, long-suffering, gentleness, goodness, faith, meekness; [and] temperance…." Another translation uses the words "patience and kindness" (NIV) instead of "long-suffering and gentleness," and "self-control" instead of "temperance." Clearly, whether old-fashioned or contemporary words are used, there is a stark contrast between the list of the works of the flesh and the fruit of the Spirit.

The Spirit that produces this good fruit is the Holy Spirit, God himself living within the person who has trusted the Lord Jesus as his or her Savior and Lord. Human effort cannot produce the fruit of love, joy, and peace. Human effort cannot produce patience and kindness, nor the other fruits listed. But God can produce this kind of good fruit in his people.

If you are a caregiver, you are probably aware of the importance of human relationships. People live in relationship to other human beings, whether family or friends or patients or caregivers. Each fruit mentioned can benefit other people.

Our Father, how we thank you that we are part of your family and that you have produced fruit in us to share with one another. Help me to faithfully share your good gifts today. Thank you for Jesus, who embodied all these qualities. Amen.

Stop for a minute. Think of each of the fruits individually and how someone else can enjoy what God is producing in you. Think about love. Think about joy. Think about peace. Think about patience or long-suffering. Think about gentleness or kindness. Meditate on goodness and faith produced in you for communication to others. Meditate on the benefits of meekness and self-control. Consider memorizing this list.

DAY 19
What Do You Want?

Whenen I was involved in my father's care at the same time that I was working full time, nearly every minute of my time was accounted for. Friends with good intentions said things like "Let me know if ever I can help...." It took me a while to learn how to ask for help. Then I found many people really are willing to be helpful, if only they know what the needs are. It was unfair for me to expect them to guess my needs or to expect them to interpret a subtle hint. I had to learn to ask directly and specifically.

READ MATTHEW 20:29–34.

It's hard to believe that Jesus didn't already know the answer when he asked the blind men, "What do you want me to do for you?" Of course the blind men said they wanted to see. But Jesus caused this to be a direct and specific encounter. No doubt Jesus had his reasons for directing these blind men to specify and give words to their need.

Various ways that Jesus healed are recorded in the Bible. Jesus knew that some people need one thing, and some another. He met people where their real needs were. Also, I think his various ways of healing were intended to teach us, as we read about these incidents years later, that it is OK to ask him for what we need and also OK to ask his people for what we need. Sometimes the way he provides can be surprising.

Dear Lord, will you please use this lesson both to teach me to ask for help, and also to prepare me to be one who gives help when I am asked to give it? I bless you Lord, for yourself and also for your people. Amen.

Stop for a minute. If you are a caregiver, your need for help is no secret. Can you make a mental list of some of the people who have been especially helpful to you? Take a moment to thank God for them.

DAY 20
Jesus Wept

*T*he verse recorded in John 11:35 is the short-
est one in the Bible: "Jesus wept." God must
have wanted us to know, these many years
later, that when he took on human flesh and walked
this earth, what he saw and what he experienced
made him sad, tearful–made him weep.

READ JOHN 11.

This whole chapter details an incident about Jesus
and his close friends, Mary, Martha, and Lazarus. You can
read it for yourself and imagine the emotions and thoughts
of the various people mentioned. Lazarus had died. His sisters mourned. Jesus raised him from the dead. Why did
Jesus weep? He knew he had the power to raise Lazarus. He

knew what he would do. Was he weeping because his friends were weeping? Was he weeping because death opposes life? It is less important to know why Jesus wept than it is to know that he did weep. He experienced emotions just as we experience emotions. He felt deeply, he hurt, he embraced emotional pain and sadness.

Another place in Scripture where Jesus' deep emotions are mentioned is in Mark 14:32–41. Jesus said, "My soul is overwhelmed with sorrow to the point of death." Then "...he fell to the ground and prayed, '...not what I will but what you will.'" These words were spoken in the Garden of Gethsemane, where Jesus prepared himself for what was soon to take place. Even though he knew both crucifixion and resurrection lay ahead, the Bible reads that he was "overwhelmed with sorrow," and in this condition fell to the ground, surrendering to his Father's will. Again, the Bible has recorded an incident that allows us to know something of the depth of Jesus' emotions. He knew how his disciples, friends, and family would grieve to see him suffer.

Lord, thank you for letting us know that it is all right to cry. You experienced human life and human death, and you reveal deep human feelings to us. Again, we thank you. Amen.

Stop for a minute. Are there tears you need to shed in company with Jesus? Share with him whatever is troubling your heart and ask him to heal your hurts. Imagine he is crying with you. Thank him for the warmth of his company and his caring.

DAY 21
Youth and Aging

*S*ome things don't change–no matter how much *we and the rest of the human race have learned or accomplished through the years.* People still get old.

READ ECCLESIASTES 12.

This passage of Scripture may be familiar to you, at least its beginning: "Remember your Creator in the days of your youth...." The verses that follow are less familiar but are a poetic and graphic description of what growing old was like *then* (2500 years ago, in the days of King Solomon) and *now.* The New International Version translation of the Bible uses these words: "...the days of trouble come and the years approach when you will say, 'I find no pleasure in them....' " Then the writer describes lessened eyesight as a time "when the sun and moon and stars grow dark. He describes our dental troubles as a time when "the grinders cease because they are few." He describes our insomnia as a time "when men rise up at the sound of birds but all their songs grow faint." The realities of growing old are described in poetic language, but are no less real.

If you are a caregiver to an older person, you are probably very much aware of the diminishing senses and abilities of the aged. It is a blessing to be aware of one's Creator and to remember our Creator in our more youthful days. But it is also a blessing for an aged person when he or she can recall with gratitude and joy the many years of God's provision and comfort.

The thrust of the Book of Ecclesiastes is that life without God is meaningless! This too is an unchanged fact, then and now, and regardless of age. Hear how this book ends, quoting this time from the King James translation: "Let us hear the conclusion of the whole matter: Fear God, and keep his commandments: for this is the whole duty of man. For God shall bring every work into judgment, with every secret thing, whether it be good, or whether it be evil" (verses 13-14).

Lord, there is much "under the sun" that is both difficult and depressing, but we depend on you and thank you for revealing to us in your Word that there is more to life than what appears "under the sun." Please direct our thoughts and prayers. Amen.

Stop for a minute. Consider what life would be like without God. Pray for someone who needs God in his or her life. If you know God, thank him for his presence in your life.

DAY 22
What Lasts?

*T*he author of the Book of Hebrews wrote in the last chapter *(13:14)*: "For here we do not have an enduring city, but we are looking for the city that is to come." Earlier *(12:26–28)* the author writes this about God's promise: "At that time his voice shook the earth, but now he has promised, 'Once more I will shake not only the earth but also the heavens.' The words 'once more' indicate the removing of what can be shaken—that is, created things—so that what cannot be shaken may remain. Therefore, since we are receiving a kingdom that cannot be shaken, let us be thankful, and so worship God acceptably with reverence and awe...."*

READ HEBREWS 12 AND 13.

Sometimes we are especially aware of the temporary nature of our surroundings. If you are a caregiver to someone who is very old, you may be especially aware of the *things* he or she has accumulated that will soon be left behind. How temporary *things* are compared with the eternity that God has promised. Even cities that look permanent are not. The Bible reminds us to concentrate not on the "now" but on what is to come.

Lord, thank you for reminding me about the important, the permanent, the enduring "things" that contrast with those things that do not last. Speak to me through your Word, the Bible, so that I can concentrate on the importance of what you say.

Stop for a minute. Think about the idea of *eternity*; think about everlasting life; think about the forever-time for which God is preparing us. Think about the Bible verse proclaiming "For God so loved the world that he gave his one and only Son, that whoever believes in him shall not perish but have eternal life" (John 3:16). Do you believe in Jesus? Thank him!

God Sees Us As Individuals

An interesting thing to notice when reading what Matthew, Mark, Luke, or John has recorded about the miraculous healings of Jesus is that no two are just alike. Sometimes Jesus touched a person. Sometimes he did not. Sometimes a person first approached him. In other situations Jesus sought out or approached the needy person first. Once when Jesus healed a person's blindness he made a mudpack with his own spit to place on the blinded eyes. In another case a blind person regained his sight gradually, first seeing people as though they were moving trees. There was a time when he instructed the healed person to show himself to the priests. Some *healed people were free to talk about their miracles; other times he cautioned them not to talk about them.*

It seems to me when I read these various stories that Jesus treated each person as an individual. He knew who needed what kind of a touch from him.

Similar concern about individual needs is indicated in St. Paul's first letter to the Thessalonians when he instructs that church to "...warn those who are idle, encourage the timid, help the weak, be patient with everyone." Idle, timid, weak—all needed different kinds of attention.

READ 1 THESSALONIANS 5:12–28.

God is so gentle and personal when he takes care of us and teaches us. If you are a caregiver you may be able to appreciate this personal touch in a special way. How many people have been in your care, and how many different approaches have you had to use when helping them. You are in good company!

Lord Jesus, thank you for every example that you left for me to follow. I ask for the power and help of your Holy Spirit to enable me to do your work in your way. Amen.

Stop for a minute. Has God given you special gifts and talents that help you to do your job well? This too is his personal touch, as he ministers to and through individual people. Think about some of your own abilities, and be thankful.

DAY 24
Doubt and Faith

*S*ometimes *when we think about the details of the story, a familiar biblical personality seems to come alive in a new way. I think of Thomas, "the doubter," who earned this nickname by his need to be convinced, to have that extra bit of evidence, perhaps to have a little more time before coming to full belief. Unless there is the possibility of doubt there is no meaning to the word* faith. *Doubt and faith often exist together, in tension with each other. The Bible states that we walk by faith, not by sight. If we could always see clearly, what need would we have for faith?*

Read John 20:24–31.

An important thing to notice when we reread Thomas's story is the fact that he showed up! He did not absent himself from the company of the other disciples. He did not hide away, mulling over his private intellectual doubts. He came to the same upper room where his believing friends had gathered. He honestly confessed his unbelief.

Thomas was faithful even while his faith was weak. He had missed an earlier meeting, but he came now to this one, and he was not disappointed. Jesus was there. Knowing Thomas's needs, Jesus said to him: "Put your finger here; see my hands. Reach out your hand and put it into my side. Stop doubting and believe." And Thomas said to him, "My Lord and my God!" His encounter was with the Lord Jesus Christ, the person whom he loved and wanted to continue to love.

If you are a caregiver, you have probably encountered any number of doubters among your patients, your colleagues, your friends. Suffering and difficulties and tense situations can contribute to doubt but can also move people toward a deeper faith.

Lord, please cause Thomas's example and experience to encourage doubters to keep coming back to the place where they still may meet you. And may believers always welcome them. Amen.

Stop for a minute. Think honestly about doubt and faith. Faith is God's gift to us. By God's grace we are saved through faith, and this is not of ourselves but is God's gift. We can always thank God for the gift of faith, and we can pray to him, asking him for more faith—more for someone else, more for ourselves.

DAY 25
Family, Not Slave

Most of St. Paul's letters that the Bible preserves for us are addressed to churches— to all the assembled Christians in places such as Rome, Corinth, Galatia, Philippi, or Thessalonica. Paul also wrote letters to individual Christian leaders, to Timothy, to Titus, and a letter with a special purpose addressed to Philemon and his friends.

Paul addresses these individuals as though they were family. Both Timothy and Titus he calls "son." Philemon's wife he calls "sister." Paul presses this idea of "church family" onto Philemon's conscience when he also refers to "my son Onesimus"—who happened to be Philemon's runaway slave. Paul goes further: Philemon now should see Onesimus "no longer as a slave, but...as a dear brother.... in the Lord."

READ ALL OF THE BOOK OF PHILEMON (IT HAS ONLY 25 VERSES).

The nature of slavery two thousand years ago in the Roman world is not Paul's subject in this letter to Philemon. Paul's subject is the attitude of one Christian toward another Christian—who is not a slave but a dear brother.

To have brothers and sisters in the Lord is like having an additional family, just as real as the human family we were born into. Caregivers are sometimes in situations where family ties are visible, sometimes strained or broken, often the subject of discussion. Family-member caregivers may be especially focused on the responsibilities and relationships within the human family. The "extended family" that describes Christian churches and fellowship groups may be able to help share caregiving responsibilities, especially when directly asked to do something specific. Sometimes a professional caregiver does her job with such care and compassion that she fills the caregiver role as though she were family.

Lord, I thank you for those who are caregivers. Bless them I pray, especially when they feel unappreciated or heavily burdened. Grant your Christian family greater compassion and sensitivity to opportunities to help. Amen.

Stop for a minute and wonder if there is a way you can refresh the heart and life and outlook of someone else, perhaps of another caregiver. Or perhaps you could be refreshed if you specifically mentioned your needs to someone else.

DAY 26
Sleeping and Waking

*I*f you are a caregiver, you may be especially aware of the blessedness of sleep. How good of God to design his world and us in such a way that each morning feels like a fresh start! Can you even imagine what it would be like if our lives were one long, long day of wakefulness? God knows that we need activity and stimulation, but God also knows we need times of rest and refreshment and renewal. The creation account in Genesis 1:5 takes us to the beginning: "...the evening and the morning were the first day" (KJV).

READ PSALMS 3, 4, AND 5.

Each of the above psalms contains some thought about sleep or waking. Can you think of prayers you might pray that are modeled on thoughts found in these psalms? We can pray day or night and in any place. This includes praying from our beds. Here are some possibilities. Based on Psalm 3: *Lord, awake or asleep, you take care of me. Help me to remember this when I am fearful or feel threatened by an enemy. Thank you that you hear and answer our prayers.* In Psalm 4:4 the psalmist says, "...when you are on your beds, search your hearts..." and in 4:8, "I will lie down and sleep in peace, for you alone, O LORD, make me dwell in safety." The following prayer might be appropriate here:

My father and my God, how good it is to know that I belong to you and that you hear me when I call to you. In the silence of the night, Lord, help me to have a good night's sleep, free from worry and at peace with you. I lay my concerns down at your feet now. I rest in the silence of the night.

Psalm 5:3 talks about waking. "Morning by morning, Oh Lord, you hear my voice. Morning by morning I lay my requests before you and wait in expectation." And so we might pray:

I want to start this day with you, my Lord, my God. I acknowledge you as my king. I want to obey your commands and walk as you direct me. And if these requests of mine line up with your plans for me, then, Lord, please grant them. May I see clearly the way you want me to go today.

Stop for a minute and thank God for the simplicity of his provision for us: night and day, sleeping and waking, the rhythms of living and being refreshed.

As you read Psalms 3, 4, and 5, pause to reflect the psalmist's words with your own prayer to God.

DAY 27
Longings

*I*f you are a caregiver, you may spend time reading the Bible for your own comfort or sometimes perhaps reading aloud to the person you are taking care of.

READ PSALM 42.

Using the old King James Version's words, this psalm begins: "As the hart panteth after the water brooks, so panteth my soul after thee, O God. My soul thirsteth for God, for the living God...." The hart is an animal that lives in arid areas, and it instinctively seeks water to stay alive.

There are times when we feel an almost unbearable longing for God, for knowing him better, for experiencing his presence and his active guidance. In reading the Bible we both partially satisfy this longing, and, paradoxically, we also stimulate and increase the longing. When we pray, the experience is similar: We both feel joy in God's presence and a longing and yearning for a deeper joy.

Sometimes it seems that a feeling of joy is part of the longing, and a feeling of longing is part of the joy we feel. To know him is to want to know him better.

Our God is so great and our expectations of eternity with him are so beyond our human comprehension that these mysterious and sometimes confusing experiences are a part of our daily walk—here and now in this world, in this life, a present hint of future heavenly fulfillment.

In the first chapter of 1 Peter, verses 1–9, the apostle Peter captures something of these feelings. He writes in 1 Peter 1:8–9, "Though you have not seen him, you love him; and even though you do not see him now, you believe in him and are filled with an inexpressible and glorious joy, for you are receiving the goal of your faith, the salvation of your souls."

The writer of the Book of Hebrews *(11:13–16)* concludes this way about God's faithful people: "...they were longing for a better country—a heavenly one. Therefore God is not ashamed to be called their God, for he has prepared a city for them." Both this writer and Peter refer to the believers as aliens and pilgrims in this present world.

Lord, Thank you for planting within me this longing for you. Amen.

Stop for a minute. If you have time, read the first chapter of 1 Peter and notice references to time and eternity and the sense of being a stranger in this world. Think about what this might mean. Ask God to guide your thoughts and prayers. Thank him for the wonderful resources we have in the Bible—such as Psalm 42, that so well describes our condition. God knows us and how we feel.

DAY 28
Obeying God's Directions

*P*hilip was one of Jesus' disciples and a leader in the early apostolic church. In the eighth chapter of the Book of Acts some incidents involving Philip are recorded. What a wonderful book of church history the Book of Acts is for us! It is an exciting book to read, any part at any time, but especially if one has an hour free and a good modern translation of the Bible, the Book of Acts can be read without interruption as an adventure story where God's Holy Spirit is the main character!

HERE IS ONE OF THE STORIES RECORDED IN
ACTS 8:26–31:

> Now an angel of the Lord said to Philip,
> "Go south to the road—the desert road—
> that goes down from Jerusalem to Gaza."
> So he started out, and on his way he met
> an Ethiopian eunuch, an important offi-
> cial in charge of all the treasury of
> Candace, queen of the Ethiopians. This
> man had gone to Jerusalem to worship,
> and on his way home was sitting in his
> chariot reading the book of Isaiah the
> prophet. The Spirit told Philip, "Go to
> that chariot and stay near it."
>
> Then Philip ran up to the chariot and
> heard the man reading Isaiah the prophet.
> "Do you understand what you are read-
> ing?" Philip asked.
>
> "How can I," he said, "unless someone
> explains it to me?" So he invited Philip to
> come up and sit with him.

The story continues with Philip explaining to the
Ethiopian how the prophet Isaiah foretold the good news
about the life and death of Jesus, and the Ethiopian's
declaring his faith and trust in Jesus and asking to be bap-
tized as a Christian. Philip was obedient to the angel's
voice to "go south" and the Holy Spirit's command to "go
to that chariot."

Lord, while I may not know your long-term will for me, I thank you that in your word, the Bible, I can come to understand the way you want me to live day by day, minute by minute, making decisions and choices as you lead me. For this wisdom and guidance, I depend on you. Amen.

Stop for a minute. At least put a bookmark at Acts 1 in your Bible. Ask God for an opportunity to read this book. Perhaps he will give you an uninterrupted hour in which you can read this wonderful book of early church history.

DAY 29
Guidance

*S*ometimes it's hard to know what to do. Our lives are filled with decisions about where to live, where to work, what to do with our time. Our lives are structured based on the decisions we have made: whom to marry, what to study in school. And our lives seem also to depend on what other people decided and did—our parents, other family members. God is in charge and he can put all these pieces together for us. Trust him!

READ PHILIPPIANS 4.

Earlier we read about how Philip, a leader in the early apostolic church, obeyed the instruction of an angel who said, "Go south to the road—the desert road—that goes down from Jerusalem to Gaza" (Acts 8:26). Then he also obeyed the leading of God's Holy Spirit, who told Philip, "Go to that chariot and stay near it" (Acts 8:29).

Because Philip was obedient to the angel's voice to "go south" and the Holy Spirit's command to "go to that chariot," he was instrumental in the Ethiopian traveler's coming to faith in Jesus Christ, followed by his baptism as a Christian believer. But what about us? Do we have such clear instructions? Without hearing the voice of an angel and without hearing the clear command of the Holy Spirit, we have to live out our daily lives as Christians step by step, one step at a time. Can we know we are living in obedience to what God wants us to do?

As a caregiver, you have been responsive to meeting someone's need. Perhaps you are caring for a family member or a good friend. Or perhaps you are employed as a professional caregiver to meet the serious and continuing needs of someone who is elderly or very ill. Whatever the circumstance, we can be thankful to God that he calls us to "walk by faith and not by sight." He knows we do not see into the future, and he knows we are not privileged to hear the voices of angels. But God has provided. He has revealed himself to us in his Word, the holy Bible. And his Word can shine light onto our paths sufficient for our walking step by step where he wants us to go. His Word also gives clear guidance about what he wants us to be.

Lord, I continue to trust you, moment by moment, to lead me. It is my desire to follow you, and I trust you to direct me in all things. Thank you for your Holy Spirit and for your Word. Amen.

Stop for a minute. Think about *Philippians 4:4-9*, which is one of many passages in Scripture that provide practical guidance on how to live. Ask for God's guidance as you make any decisions, both the important and big decisions and the more ordinary and seemingly less important decisions.

DAY 30
Mentoring

W hen we read chapter 4 of 1 Timothy, the first of two books St. Paul wrote to his young friend and colleague, we find it full of practical advice. Paul was like a mentor to Timothy, communicating to him by both example and words some of the things he needed to know in order to be an effective local church leader. How should a church organize to best honor God and serve its members and declare the good news of the gospel to outsiders? How should Timothy prioritize his interests and activities? In a way Timothy was a caregiver—providing oversight and care to "his flock," the Christian believers who were in his church and looking to him *for leadership. And Paul provided similar oversight and care to Timothy.*

READ 1 TIMOTHY 4.

Although specifically addressed to Pastor Timothy, there is much in the Books of 1 Timothy and 2 Timothy that is instructive for all of us. When you have time you may want to read both of these short books. For now, let's concentrate on 1 Timothy 4. Here are some of the verses as they read in the New International Version (NIV) of the Bible. Verses 1 through 5 caution Timothy (and us) to be aware that not everything is true! Some notions that we encounter are deceptive and demonic. Test what you hear by comparing it to what the Bible teaches, and avoid false teaching. Sometimes false teaching takes the form of restrictions and prohibitions, like abstaining from good foods that—as Paul writes—"God created to be received with thanksgiving by those who believe and who know the truth. For everything God created is good, and nothing is to be rejected if it is received with thanksgiving, because it is consecrated by the word of God and prayer."

In verses 6 and following, Paul encourages Timothy to "...train yourself to be godly. For physical training [or exercise] is of some value, but godliness has value for all things, holding promise for both the present life and the life to come."

Physical exercise has limited value; spiritual exercise has eternal value! Timothy is told to "Command and teach these things...set an example for the believers in speech, in life, in love, in faith and in purity...Be diligent in these matters; give yourself wholly to them, so that everyone may see your progress. Watch your life and doctrine closely. Persevere in them, because if you do, you will save both yourself and your hearers."

Lord Jesus, be my Mentor! And use others and use me to spread your word.

Stop for a minute. Read as much of 1 Timothy as you have time to. Think of older people who have mentored you. Is there practical guidance that you use as a caregiver that you have gained from what a mentor has taught you? Are you in the role of mentor to some younger person? Pray that you may influence that person toward a life of thankfulness and godliness.

DAY 31
Remembering God

The Book of Deuteronomy recaps the early history of Israel and warns appropriately. This book also warns the readers, like you and me, to think about our own tendency to drift away from God. Not only do I read about the ways ancient Israel drifted into idolatry, but I see how I suffer the same weakness and share the same tendency. I read the warnings to Israel to remember God, and I recognize my need to heed these warnings, for we share the same temptation to erroneously claim self-sufficiency.

READ DEUTERONOMY 8.

Here are some verses selected from *Deuteronomy 8*, using the New International Version of the Bible, the NIV, with the words "remember" or "forget" italicized:

> *Remember* how the LORD your God led you all the way in the desert these forty years, to humble you and to test you in order to know what was in your heart, whether or not you would keep his commands... When you have eaten and are satisfied, praise the LORD your God for the good land he has given you. Be careful that you *do not forget* the LORD your God, failing to observe his commands, his laws and his decrees that I am giving you this day. Otherwise, when you eat and are satisfied, when you build fine houses and settle down, and when your herds and flocks grow large and your silver and gold increase and all you have is multiplied, then your heart will become proud and *you will forget* the LORD your God, who brought you out of Egypt, out of the land of slavery...You may say to yourself, "My power and the strength of my hands have produced this wealth for me." But *remember* the LORD your God, for it is he who gives you the ability to produce wealth,

and so confirms his covenant, which he
swore to your forefathers, as it is today.

And finally, the serious warning in verse 19: "If
you ever *forget* the LORD your God and follow other gods
and worship and bow down to them, I testify against you
today that you will surely be destroyed."

Thank you, Lord, for all you have provided
throughout my life. These good things come from your good
hand, not my own ability or intelligence. I praise and thank
you! Amen.

Stop for a minute. If you are a caregiver, you very
likely have had contact with all kinds of people. How
sweet it is when we hear a person give praise and
thanks to God for the blessings he or she has
enjoyed. How can you help communicate that sweet-
ness?

AND ONE DEVOTION
FOR EVERY DAY...
People/Joy

*T*wo Scripture passages are suggested here on the subject of joy. One is from the letter identified as 3 John, a short letter that the apostle John wrote to a Christian friend named Gaius. John's hearing news about his faithful friend gave him great joy. The other Scripture verses are scattered throughout Philippians, a letter the apostle Paul wrote to the Christians at Philippi.

READ 3 JOHN 1–4 AND PHILIPPIANS (AS LISTED BELOW).

It was Christmastime, and we had just sung the carol, "Joy to the world, the Lord is come...." and my mind turned to thoughts about joy. Joy (which has to do with our condition) is something deeper than happiness (which has more to do with what's happening). I wanted to imagine new or added ways of "enjoying the joy" that the Bible promises. Because we are aware of so much pain and unhappiness and trouble, often the idea of "joy" is not immediately evident.

In the Book of Philippians, Paul uses the word "joy" a lot. In the dozen or so places where joy or gladness are mentioned in this book, more than half connect joy with other believers. In 1:3 and 4 the memories of and prayers for believers gave Paul joy. In 1:26 it was being present with one another. In 2:2 it was their unity and unselfishness. In 2:17 and 18 it was their shared lives and shared suffering. In 2:29 it was the joy of receiving a brother in the Lord. In 4:1 it was the firmness of their faith.

I concluded that to know greater joy, God wants me to reach out more to my brothers and sisters in Christ, to know and appreciate them, and to enjoy them, to spend less time alone and more time with others. And the mirror of this thought is that I should tailor my life in Christ to be sure it can be a source of joy to other believers!

If you are a caregiver, you know how important people are. We live in community and in contact with other people, and so we should. We are made this way, and these relationships can be channels for the flow of joy.

Dear Lord, open my life to better include others, and in the give and take of human relationships, to be able to give and receive joy. Thank you for these possibilities.

Stop for a minute. If you have time and if you don't mind marking your Bible, underline the many times the words "joy" or "gladness" or "enjoy" appear in Philippians. Think about the things that have given you joy and thank God for them.

ILLUMINATIONBOOKS

Other Books in the Series

Everyday Virtues
by *John W. Crossin, OSFS*

The Mysteries of Light
by *Roland J. Faley, TOR*

Healing Mysteries
by *Adrian Gibbons Koester*

Carrying the Cross with Christ
by *Joseph T. Sullivan*

Saintly Deacons
by *Deacon Owen F. Cumming*

Finding God Today
by *E. Springs Steele*

Hail Mary and Rhythmic Breathing
by *Richard Galentino*

The Eucharist
by *Joseph M. Champlin*

Gently Grieving
by *Constance M. Mucha*